From the observer to the observed

By Márquez Price

Dedication

To the creator- for these words do not come from me, but through me. Allow me to stay aligned within your will.

To my parents- words can't describe what you mean to me. That would be a book in itself. Thank you for EVERYTHING.

Table of Contents

Bamboo

She weighed one pound,

13 ounces,

and would remain in the NICU for 96 days.

Heavy hearts,

and heightened worry seized her family,

but their collective love cocooned around her,

and she would butterfly break through with an unmatched metamorphosis of resilience.

Now,

she's the pretty girl with long bamboo limbs,

dazzling braids,

or twin afro puffs as her tiara —

 a pyramid sized heart,

and a quasar resplendent smile.

Like bamboo,

she is fast-growing.

Like bamboo,

she used her compressive strength that is greater than brick,

concrete,

and wood to carry the load of daunting odds,

and survived.

Like bamboo,

she uses the tensile strength,

that matches steel to stretch whenever circumstantially challenged.

Of bamboo essence,

I nicknamed my niece Bamboo.

Barry Sanders

I remember watching this guy run with the football,

with my simultaneous introduction to quantum physics —

he was as quick as teleportation,

with a smorgasbord of elusive moves,

that lost tackles like yesterday,

and sometimes he'd also lose 10 yards,

before gaining 15 on the same play.

He was as unpredictable,

and exciting as anyone witnessed on a football field,

to me,

and somehow,

the recollection of his gift carrying the ball,

and my thoughts at the chance of carrying your heart the same,

became an interpolation of the steps my imagination made into the manifestation of us.

Infinite

I once knew a brave man,

willing to go his entire life —

to prove that his staying power would outlast any neophyte,

in the regions of her psyche,

because his certainty was seeded in his memory of her from before —

they say the sands under our feet,

equal the stars as far as our eyesight can reach at night,

so,

I navigated the doors of time,

and optimism,

between grains of people throughout galaxies —

to find you with the hands of infinity in my favor.

Good Juju

I remember to dispense kindness,

patience,

and understanding —

from a reservoir I keep,

when traveling through disparate worlds of idiosyncrasies
inhabited by others,

because the ancestors of West Africa taught me —

that treating others how you want to be treated,

is good Juju,

in an existence of one large organism of people.

Bodies

Snapshots of nostalgia,

that boy had a fire crackle cackle,

and cracked jokes that lit laughter like the 4th of July —

we were his audience,

the classroom his stage.

On the court he could spin like D. Rose,

or Pearl Monroe —

not left hand to his right direction,

or right hand to his left direction —

but right to right,

and left to left,

I mimicked his move into my repertoire —

twirls of a whirling dervish,

a pivot patterned after his father's movement away from the
impressionable stage of his life.

It takes moxie to be magnanimous,

but a kid can't reconcile sleep for dinner,

and an absentee father fading further into the distance like
an apparition.

Fast forward —

You hear ol' boy got out?

Sometimes a cage facilitates the monster within —

one exasperated by your words of *rehabilitation.*

With several bullets,

he desecrated her compassion,

concern,

and wings reserved for flight to where angels fly effortlessly —

precipitated by a salvo of accusations,

the street scuttlebutt sang that his brother is still missing —

the national news reported,

that the bodies he caught along his path of annihilation are still being found —

a mother murdered by a son when she was given word that he might be a serial killer,

and confronted one.

Archenemy

Fear of abandonment,

and trust,

were opposite ends of a shoestring,

that I laced,

and tied together,

tightly on a shoe I wore to walk through relationships with others —

but when that shoe wore out,

and I realized blame for external reasons,

equaled my lack of growth —

Lex Luthor,

The Joker,

Green Goblin,

and Megatron disappeared —

and I saw that my archenemy was me.

Periodic table

Sometimes I feel small—

like the point at which the pin is pushed through the map to show a mere spot on the globe.

Billions of years ago,

there was a star that shone splendid,

before my eyes could see it,

yet,

my elevator of belonging rises—

when I understand that nearly all the elements in the human body,

were made from that same star.

Oneness

Human connection is so astounding,

that loneliness can be alleviated by a stranger if you allow yourself to be open.

An intuitive nod that gives another solace when danger lurks —

a guffaw from a group of people,

rendered incapable of resisting something humorous,

and simultaneous,

initiated,

fading moments,

that adorn the tapestry of people with power —

refusing the pull of divisiveness as an indolent alternative.

The Golden Rule

The city buildings assist,

as a charcoal sketch of a dreary skyline —

workers pass by the unkempt maverick daily on a divergent
path.

Sometimes downtrodden with his head down,

he avoids eye contact with the melancholic melodies of Lady
Day in each step of his saunter,

but flip the page on the calendar,

and he appears rabid —

frothing at the mouth,

cussing and hollering —

pigeons clearing paths as he weaves in,

and out of downtown labyrinthine streets,

and alleys.

Adolescents point and laugh,

but they wouldn't if they saw the boy rendition of this man
in '89 —

when the crack epidemic was at its pinnacle,

and every Friday night his father,

and card playing cronies got high off their own supply,

and would compete wildly for first place —

the prize was to take advantage of the boy in the bathroom
until he ran away,

his violators escaping with impunity,

and his development arrested to what felt punitive with placement—

in group homes that housed rounds of fist fights,

juvenile detention stints,

and an addiction to shooting a horse that runs as hard as the Kentucky Derby,

through his veins when he releases it from the tip of a needle—

stories unknown,

because sometimes when he feels good enough to try at a decent day,

I witness a familiar scene,

where he stands bedraggled,

and still,

with parched skin matching his traverse beaten shoes—

another passerby impugned him with the condescending,

"Get a job,"

instead of exchanging humanity,

and compassion,

when the man humbled himself enough to ask for change—

maybe not change in coins,

but in the behavior of how we overlook each other's pain.

Feng Shui

Over 7 billion people on the planet,

and throughout the course of my life,

a sense of being blanketed by the population has always been present,

but I realized that a daunting 7 billion can pale in comparison to the absence of one,

when I saw that your toothbrush was gone,

and the basic principles of Feng Shui commenced at my place.

If, for a day...

If,

for a day,

you could wear my skin –

you would see how I am part of the most marginalized,

and misunderstood group in the western world.

You would understand why I am culturally conditioned to be stoic,

strong,

and somehow get labeled as 'angry'

because I don't feel like squeezing into your cultural appropriations,

so that you can feel comfortable –

I learned to make a mask out of my flat,

facial affect,

long before Covid19 deemed it necessary for survival,

and being that you would know what it feels like to be expendable –

you wouldn't ask me why blacks are killing blacks in Chicago if you were colonized,

and tempered to hate yourself in an impoverished environment that obstructs your vision –

of hope,

and a future,

with a frayed psyche to kill your own kind –

any race of people pitted against itself in such a setting of iniquity,

have proven to kill each other the same.

It isn't an excuse gambit,

don't be obtuse.

You would see how it feels to be profiled unjustly,

stopped,

searched,

and how fear flies high with the sound of that blue and red siren,

seeding itself in your DNA long before you hear it.

You would know what systemic racism is,

when your wings of ambition are bound to your sides,

and freedom starts to resemble something mythical.

You wouldn't ask me why I run so fast,

because you'd understand what it feels like to run twice as fast,

but to only get half as far in America.

You'd understand my indifference,

towards being invited to a gathering where I'm not the predominate,

but the tag along token —

sometimes I want to be around my own,

naked of the costume you need me to wear to feel comfortable in your own skin.

You'd understand how being a contrarian at times is a symptom of my plight, and mechanism used —

to remind you not to get too common with me,

because I know when you haven't taken the time to understand me,

from a lazy position of privilege.

You'd understand that when you say,

"You talk white"

when I display my intelligence,

that I am not imitating whiteness —

as intelligence is not an inherently white trait.

Nor would you render my intelligence to my usage of colloquial euphemisms,

nah mean?

Because if you think of it,

I'm a linguistic genius,

after being stripped of my dialect to master your English.

You'd understand that 30 seconds of a curriculum in *his*tory,

and a month out of a year is not a fair exchange for reparations —

because when you learn that the history of reparation payments for us equals zero,

your eyes squint to a peruse.

It reads at the bottom of the chart —

United States of America,

from 1865 to present,

Slavery and Jim Crow era,

African American Black Descendants.

But,

If for a day,

You could wear my skin –

you'd know,

that during the creation process,

our tissue is borrowed from our mother's body,

and every time you touch your skin,

you are not only touching your mother,

but you are touching your grandmother,

and the first mother.

Life recycles,

and we are our ancestors.

The eyes of Lucy,

have watched how skin relegates humanity from Ethiopia for 3.2 billion years—

before **black** was a description for a people to be subjugated by,

or something you thought you could be more of than me,

because you have a bigger collection of Jordan's,

you'd know that none of that,

is our origin—

If,

For a day,

You'd understand.

Shaka Zulu

Peace king—

the video of your last physical moments here transfixed,

and traumatized me—

my seethe became an unbridled fury.

The blood in my eyes couldn't see the peace,

that normally lubricates my vision.

The way they stalked,

and murdered you,

enlisted me to a war to defend against those cowards who trespassed your body.

I wanted to summon Shaka Zulu,

and his retributive brutality—

how have we forgotten his ways that improved warfare methods in times like this,

so that we are no longer defenseless?

Your middle name is my first name,

and that namesake will be carried by me through the breath that will speak words—

to pancake hatred upon impact,

like a hollow point from the chamber of my mind—

endless rounds fired for your defended honor.

You fought to the very end,

a paragon of a warrior—

your instinct was not to surrender,

but to survive.

Through two rounds,

you kept moving forward,

until the motion of your body gave out,

collapsed —

and an indelible horror pressed repeat in my head.

That was the last video I'll ever watch of a black man being cut down.

You should have never been put in that situation,

and though painful to accept,

I can't help but to be proud of how you fought through impossible odds.

The collective spirit of our ancestors was channeled,

they can't kill us all —

and you will live on.

Ahmaud Arbery.

Samson

I was irate for that kid,

Andrew Johnson,

like Samson surrounded by Delilah,

and the philistines,

forced to cut his dreadlocks before a wrestling match in New
Jersey —

robbed of his strength,

head bowed,

humiliated.

I had sympathy for the ant —

when that kid plucked its antenna,

from its head,

for amusement on the playground,

Ms. so and so had just taught us —

that those elbowed feelers were for the ant to smell,

touch,

taste,

touch,

and communicate with other ants,

essential —

like our hair is essential to us,

Andrew Johnson,

as carbonated beings,

ether.

Gathered information in our hair connects us to our environment of nature,

like the ant,

afros look like trees,

locs like branches,

and vines —

our hair is alive,

and helped us escape —

cornrows served as maps on scalps,

long before style —

sacred geometric patterns,

for others to free ourselves from captivity.

The only people on the planet with hair that grows vertically,

Andrew Johnson,

and defies gravity like a plant —

shaved his antenna,

that absorbs the most vitamin D from the sun,

stores information,

and is an extension of our nervous system.

Andrew Johnson,

they cut your hair,

I grew mine out even more —

to be the so and so to spread the lesson,

of our hair.

Surrender

I once had a woman,

tell me that she would go to war *for* me —

and at that moment,

impregnable walls to a fortress fell —

I sheathed every weapon used before in innumerable battles,

because I realized I no longer needed to wage war within myself —

for she had conquered my hesitation with an undying ambition of love.

Sesame Street

The most dangerous neighborhood to visit,

makes Skid Row look like Sesame Street—

where doubt is the size of Big Bird,

telling you over,

and over,

like Count von Count—

that you can't advance from the poverty of your thoughts,

it'll make you Grover blue if you listen,

the chatter prattles on like Bert and Ernie,

chomps down on the peace of the neighborhood,

with the voracity of the Cookie Monster—

I slowed to a Snuffleupagus pace when I stayed too long,

and became Oscar the Grouch to my surroundings,

I had to read a sign the color of Elmo,

to stop,

and leap out with the hops of Kermit the Frog,

for the Two-Headed Monster is my ears,

and the neighborhood not to reside in is the one between them.

ASÉ

I honor my ancestors,

by prevailing in the face of adversity.

In order to break free from the shackles of depression,

I called upon them.

Cottage Cheese and Nectarine

My dad has taken to a bowl of cottage cheese,

with diced nectarine,

for years —

an invariable routine.

It's an inimitable trait within his exampled commitment to
something imperative,

that nourishes his well-being,

and in that —

I understand the woman I chose to commit to,

must do the same for me,

and vice versa —

Like cottage cheese,

and nectarine.

Sirens

She was tall like a mopane tree in southern Africa,

lissome in her sequences of movement,

paired with fervor through inordinate hours in the studio,

a dancer.

Wu Tang,

she could recite bars line for line from the Clan —

Hip-hop became our daily symposium,

in the hallways of high school,

and remained the conduit throughout the years for us to exchange —

beats,

rhymes,

albums-

the discography of our friendship,

but I've never heard a more seizing lyric,

then when I was told the father of your son —

employed the skullduggery,

to convince you to let your son go to the neighbor's house so you could talk to him —

a discussion you didn't anticipate would involve bullets,

and sirens —

alerting your 5-year-old son,

that he was now a motherless child,

with a father on his way to prison for taking your life.

Words learned when dealing with bullies

The triple digit days served as the signal,

because the unbearable heat,

somehow made him deranged,

and when the bottom of that bottle was upside down facing the ceiling fan,

it meant that he had alcohol in his system —

from his heels to the top of his warped brain matter.

The baby was sleep,

when her mother told her father that she couldn't do it anymore.

His drunken fit turned kinetic energy,

rushing towards,

and pinning her up against the refrigerator —

but she was tired,

of it,

him,

and undaunted —

looked him straight in his eyes,

and said,

"Hit me, I am untouchable."

His hands fell to his sides —

words learned when dealing with bullies,

he woke up the next morning on the sofa,

his girlfriend,

and daughter,

free.

Evolutionary, 2016.

2016.

The lowest time of my life.

Survived the tail end of '15 broke,

unemployed,

with a clunky car that broke down again—

walked home to find an eviction notice on my door,

and that cunning pack rat in my apartment I couldn't catch.

The beginning scene of 2016 started like the ending of that superhero movie—

where the villain snapped his fingers at the end,

and all the good guys started disappearing—

my friend's young corpse snug in a casket,

another headed to the penitentiary for a long stretch—

sucked back in by the vacuum of recidivism.

If I wrote down everything that happened,

that I'll never scribe,

or tell,

you'd understand that that year was a 5-year plan,

in preparation to survive a future pandemic that the common person never saw coming.

A rope of depression tied to My ankles,

connected to the fin of a whale,

plunging downward through the ocean of despair.

Try to explain to the people you love why it appears as if you're moving like a turtle,

when they ask if everything is ok—

because your smile is as weak as branch water when they study your facial features,

and the answered truth to their questioning would shatter the disguise you've manufactured,

to hide,

and survive.

It's amazing how we sabotage ourselves so not to amplify the worry of others.

Imagine going to sleep on a mattress,

that felt like quicksand in the morning when you tried to peel yourself off it,

in the eye of a perfect storm—

unconditional meets unrequited in every facet of your life,

no matter how strong the determination,

Sisyphus,

and that boulder—

the moment you realize doing everything right doesn't equate to life being fair.

2016.

It took me back to that time when me and my high school girlfriend argued,

about that very thing about life being fair,

or not—

how I couldn't admit that she was right,

in that sometimes it isn't,

and a couple of years later,

irony would display its sense of humor in college,

when I tried to understand why she was telling me she was
a lesbian after four years —

my wince wasn't at the orientation she revealed,

that I supported over what I wanted —

my wince was at what I saw in the rearview mirror,

in questioning if the road we traveled together was real —

last words of *I wanted to marry you,*

and *I wanted you to be the mother of my kids* —

my graduation plans revealed that dropped tears from her
eyes the size of avocadoes,

and it stayed with me as women in the future felt like a game
of charades,

when I looked at them —

until I was imitating faces,

and motions,

to be recognized by someone special who had lost trust in
me —

my lack of trust,

that wouldn't allow me to put my guard down,

attracted the like,

for the behavior I used in a game of tag to outmaneuver,

put me on the other side of what I swore would never catch
me —

for losing trust from someone else is like knowing you are gold,

but now they see you as silver,

and you get buried in doubt—

because even gold must be unearthed again by other hands to shine undeniably,

from a forgotten cemetery where it never loses its luster.

2016.

It took me back to that teenager who loved basketball more than anything,

but his gifts on the court were too big for a city with an antiquated mentality,

because I was the city's best kept secret on the west coast,

with a former All-American father—

attending his alma mater looking to repeat history of state championship glory.

It was where I learned how sickening jealousy can be.

Cassius and Brutus conspired in all forms—

friends,

even my best friend, teammates,

some of my own coaches,

parents of teammates,

and other players when I tried to transfer schools—

it's why I never listened to people saying I'd be a great coach down the line,

due to fear of accidently,

potentially,

disrupting a kid's dream —

but they never broke my love for that game,

nor the love between a father and a son —

he rose like the Phoenix,

and I tunneled my way through Shawshank to reach Zihuatanejo.

2016.

Thank God I was born with a blend of fierce competitiveness,

indominable will,

and my mother's voice to encourage as an emollient when adversity started to peel my skin —

because it got me back up towards the end of 2016,

but it was propelled by anger until I was stark raving mad —

a conflagration ready to set everything ablaze in my path,

and I started to —

steamrolling towards retribution,

to engage a world my audacious pride swelled up to challenge,

until I pulled out one of my favorite books, and re-read it,

the tale of a man —

marooned in the dank conditions of solitary confinement,

stripped of everything for years,

until enmity,

and fate —

became the odd couple that freed him to riches beyond his wildest imagination, but his loathing hung over the wounds he still harbored after arriving at his freedom,

because —

like his mind that was never incarcerated while his body was caged,

that same mind was still in bondage,

since he didn't release his resentment after his body escaped bondage —

and in that,

Edmond Dantes reminded me,

that I was vehemently denying the sum of some of my own decisions,

of recent years,

as depression is anger turned inward,

and the timing became impeccable to try again,

repeatedly until I saw massive change in myself —

as a wise man changes,

and a fool changes naught.

What others did to you in past,

that had more to do with them than you,

and what you did to yourself in response in the future,

does not determine how you can wield your own power to be what you want now.

I worked diligently to rewire my mind for lasting results,

and I did —

evolve.

Roots

Say thank you,

to the bad,

and good experiences —

gratitude becomes the shield,

that allows you to be impervious to the clash of the outcome —

for complaints,

are cousins to the carping,

that only make you perishable,

when connected to the root of your chosen mindset.

Mr. October

I became a Yankee fan,

from an old man,

jersey with number 44,

he wore—

sittin' on his porch listening to games on the radio,

walking by on my way from school,

he'd look up from his radio and say,

keep swingin' —

then years later it made sense,

keep swingin' —

through the failed attempts,

your resilience,

is the unconquerable enemy used to swing when life pitches hardships—

keep swingin'-

sometimes you'll swing,

and miss,

keep swingin' —

I connected the number 44,

he wore,

to the player it represented,

who finished with more strikeouts than hits,

but hit homeruns when it counted,

Keep swingin' —

whatever obstacle,

or setback he faced,

he bounced back,

Keep swingin' —

they 'own' the pitchers,

in how they walk up to the plate,

and therefore,

the key to the hitter lies in the boldness,

like Reggie Jackson,

long before I'd be born in October,

and he'd be given the nickname of the 10th month,

Keep swingin'-

that old man was putting a battery of confidence in my back —

I've worn a Yankee cap ever since.

Rosetta Stone

Sometimes I act like I can't hear you,

and you repeat yourself —

my subterfuge surmounts your innocence once again.

I teased my sisters incessantly as boy,

and with you,

I get to be the child at play again.

I just wanted to hear your thick accent try to squeeze,

and get stuck,

between the gates of phonetics —

you wag your finger at me,

and we laugh.

"Habla mi idioma"

and that's exactly what I'll do,

To get closer to you.

The Ant and the Octopus

Brotha man,

if you want to survive as a unit,

study the ant—

his community is his colony,

their communication with each other is adroit,

with an ability to solve complicated problems.

These parallels,

Have long been a revelation of study with many human societies—

they've studied you,

and you haven't studied yourself.

Brotha man,

if you want to survive alone,

study the octopus—

learn to squeeze through the compact gaps of your habitat,

with a complex nervous system,

and superb sight to see what is seen,

and unseen—

intelligent,

and behaviorally diverse—

because it will feel like you need 8 limbs to swim.

Strategize to defend yourself against predators—

camouflage,

displays of threat,

and be venomous if you must,

for you have been seen as sea monsters since mythology —

brotha man,

survive.

Tribe

The quieter I am,

the more I can hear.

Mahalia Jackson greeted you at the door of my grandmother's house back then—

my father asked her when he was the age I am now,

what it was like when she was his age,

"Every day was like Sunday,"

She said,

and that's when dinner was served for all the family.

My grandfather swung his arms when he walked,

and miles his feet took him during the Odyssey of his life,

became the stories my father would recite—

validating that his old man was everything to him,

and a man I wished I had met.

I went from being the observer,

to being the observed,

overnight—

asking for greatness doesn't always meet the unanticipated warp speed at which it arrives,

and I am grateful,

because they say a man can't be a prophet in his own town—

but I reminisce,

when my maternal grandfather,

took me and my twin cousins,

with my uncle,

to fishing trips—

where I caught my first fish,

and put it back in the lake,

because I somehow knew that what I caught didn't belong
to me,

and that allowing others to do the same is the utmost
courtesy.

It was those times that would expand like the ripples
beneath the boat,

and now resurface at the dock of today,

to assure me that all I need to do is close my eyes,

be humble,

and listen—

to the tribe that prepared me for this day since I was born.

1st meeting

She said she had the fuel of a million cynical women running
through her veins —

but that her daughter will grow up kind,

curious,

and happy —

and if she decides that she wants to know her dad,

she will,

and can ask the questions herself —

because within the foresight of her protective nature,

she won't taint the image of the father,

that her daughter never knew.

Bondage

We bullhorn our freedoms,

at every preconceived notion of an entity encroaching —

but the soreness in our necks,

from heads that genuflect,

to technological servitude,

say otherwise —

a bondage bequeathed to our children yearning for our attention,

and learning to imitate our intimacy bereft interactions with each other.

Addition

Anonymous one was mercurial.

He changed with every fad of prepubescence—

Dickie suit,

and a raider's hat for gangsta rap,

when the west coast,

was the dress code.

The next week—

on the periphery of skater association,

when fat laces took flight with airborne twisting boards,

for wheels to land on scuffed concrete,

leaving sharpie looking marks on sidewalks—

it matched the unpredictability of his homelife,

where the stoicism of his mother bewildered his attempts to bond,

and his father amused himself by driving up humungous hills,

only to cover his eyes,

and face,

with his hands,

at the apex of those hills,

forcing anonymous one to grab the steering wheel,

as the car zigzagged down towards awaiting peril—

the conditions that came to puppeteer his aloof nature,

making him appear to be suspended in oddness,

unable to be pulled by the strings of failed engagement by
his peers,

but somehow,

we linked through levity —

a mutual affinity for episodes of Martin brought us back
together,

throughout the years in revisited laughter.

Anonymous two was as loyal as they come.

I met him in the bathroom one day in high school,

when some upperclassmen tried to jump him.

"Bro, I'll kill for you if anyone ever tries to fuck with you
from this day forward."

I thought his statement was hyperbolic,

but the kid I joined to rescue from an uneven ratio of a sneak
ambush,

engraved his words in a bond —

and when I'd see him on Mondays in class,

I'd ask why he looked so tired,

until one day he rolled up his sleeve,

and showed me tracks —

where his father would puncture holes with needles,

for Heroin to course through his veins,

and gooey his inhibitions,

on weekends across the border when he needed his son to a
be a soldier —

in a drug war,

anonymous two made bodies drop from rapid AK47 gun fire,

hanging out the window of a car driven by his father,

with a right hand on the steering wheel,

and left-hand spraying terror at enemies brave enough to see if they had a maker,

to meet.

Anonymous two found a way to escape the weekends when he met his girlfriend —

she was the only thing that made sense to him,

he stuck to her like a sole on a shoe,

for grounding,

when his past evoked thoughts of potential tempestuous streaks —

for years until got he caught up on some drug offenses,

and was sentenced to 5 years.

I ran into anonymous one at a party in college.

He had dropped out of high school,

but had been working a steady job since.

Told me he met this girl who ditched her boyfriend when he got sent up to serve time.

His name was Anonymous two.

"This sucka keeps calling collect and threatening me,

but I told his ass we can get busy when gets out."

I tried to caution anonymous one about anonymous two,

but his hubris put an S on his chest —

he didn't realize this was no comic book.

All seasons of Martin were finished,

and this wasn't funny.

A year later —

to the date that I saw anonymous one,

I heard anonymous two was shot,

and killed at the border in a failed escape from the country,

48 hours after he was released from prison.

Two bodies were found in the back of a building with bullets
in both heads,

anonymous one and his girlfriend.

It didn't take mathematics to figure out that —

one plus two,

equals anonymous.

Gingerbread man

You kept trying to get me to rap like you,

but your command of speaking cadence was innate.

You showed me how to dunk as a diminutive hooper,

we hurdled hurdles on the grass doing plyometrics.

Sometimes I visit that gym —

haven't played there in so long,

because that metal bench is still there —

the one I was lacing up my shoes on,

and waiting for you to pull up at for Saturday morning
run —

when I was met by news instead,

that you were in your bathtub with a shotgun on your lap,

she had left you —

and you had committed suicide.

I think at 14 years old was the first time,

that the idea of commitment to someone else scared me,

because I thought people stayed together forever like the
movies —

I created the ability to not show my feelings too much,

and run,

like the gingerbread man —

because people who love hard,

have the tendency to lose sense of self,

when met with unrequited.

It took me years to let the gingerbread man go,

because it's safe when you love yourself,

and the person you love,

loves themselves.

Circus

Social media is a circus.

Clowns,

crowds,

and outlandish exhibits.

You're either a consumer purchasing a ticket,

or a buyer investing in the hoopla.

The ghost of P.T. Barnum still knows a gullible audience makes a profit.

I found out a way to monetize the circus,

because my attendance there reminded me,

that attention,

and time,

are currencies you shall not waste,

on social media.

Change

They say the 5 closest people to you,

are who you are,

and to determine the priorities of those 5 people as quickly as you can.

If it's gluttony,

we will help each other to a buffet of health issues —

amazing how we kill animals,

and eat dead flesh,

when it eventually kills us for eating it.

If it's gossip,

we will speak of others,

and not to each other —

a perfect way to stifle undivided understanding.

If it's laziness,

we will slow time down,

and waste our lives together.

If it's hatred,

we will calcify as rock,

inanimate to the limbs of life that allow us to move away from the frequency of fear.

But if it's self-accountability,

we will form a fist,

from 5 fingers,

able to swing,

and knock over the barriers that stymie our ability to change ourselves,

and the world.

Genie

Spoke to a genie,

she said she'd grant me 3 wishes.

Told her I'd like 3 things to prepare me for fatherhood.

A niece,

A niece,

And a nephew soon followed.

Spider-Woman

I saw a woman with these eyes —
and when they contacted mine,
an epiphany came to light,
and I realized for the first time,
what the paralysis of the fly is like,
when it's stuck in the web of its captor.

Shootin' dice

I think we like to shoot dice,

not because it excites —

we're cupping,

shaking,

talkin' shit,

musterin' up courage,

and throwing —

the probability to a wind,

in this gambling shack we know as life,

that we know can blow our conditions as black men —

in any erratic direction,

by the time those same dice hit the concrete —

to reveal numbers that determine our wins,

and loses.

100

An old soldier,

country boy from Mississippi,

cantankerous long before his later decades,

it was his makeup—

coffee straight,

black as asphalt,

every morning for breakfast.

He chewed tobacco,

and slept with that German Mauser under his pillow,

till the day that he died—

sometimes,

I thought his mean nature was the fuel that pushed his lifespan so long,

but he had a smile that was disarming—

"Oh me,"

he'd say when he'd laugh,

it was infectious—

and he was there,

when you were a grandchild with chicken pox,

or in need of a place to stay,

when being grown,

was a premature advance on the real world.

I saw generational wealth clearer,

when he openly talked about inheritance,

and emphasized the wishes of his house to never be sold.

He never worried about anything,

and his will power was as strong as anyone—

but his last offering of wisdom to me was that,

we are not in control,

he wanted to reach 100,

and left at 99 years,

and 10 months,

2 months from his birthdate.

6 feet tall

Fate said —

you'll never be 6 feet,

but rather multiple fathoms deep,

when you speak,

with words able to flood minds when they enter them —

the thoughts written down on tall pieces of paper,

are cut in half when the machete swings,

but the same piece of paper dulls the machete when submerged in water —

tall,

like 6 feet,

or deep,

like fathoms,

6 feet,

each.

P.I.M.P

A child has no guile,

and numbers don't lie,

but any man,

or woman,

who will manipulate —

with a carrot,

and stick shtick,

of an exchange,

between your offering in the form of a belief,

and money,

is equivalent to a —

Preacher Infiltrating Minds Persuasively.

Sisters

I got sisters who changed my diapers,

sisters I shared a room with,

sisters obsessed with Prince,

and Maxwell—

posters all over the walls,

and songs on repeat for hours.

Sisters who looked after me,

like additional mothers,

they helped raise me.

Sisters who used to wear the thickest of coke bottle glasses,

sisters who used to practice the running ran in the living room for hours.

Sisters who put me on their lap while driving a booger-green Datsun,

sisters who dropped me off at the movies to meet with girls,

sisters who let me drive their Nissan when I got my license—

I went speeding around a corner one day until it spun out of control,

four furious times before it shut off,

I gathered myself,

and never told.

Sisters I would squirt with water guns,

and stick my finger under their nose while they tried to sleep—

sisters with patience,

I teased,

and terrorized,

they answered the call every time I needed help.

Sisters I fought with in the morning,

commiserated with by the afternoon.

Sisters I've traveled coast to coast with,

Cail to chocolate city.

Sisters I went to church with,

Sunday dinners,

and family reunions.

Sisters I probably laugh the hardest with,

than anyone else,

when we get going on something funny,

shared memories-

stories that are inextricably woven into the fabric of my consciousness.

Sisters who are different than me,

but the same.

Sisters no matter what,

I'd find a way to reconcile with—

an unspoken vow I made long ago to my parents,

I'd surrender before I'd allow them to see us hampered by our petty differences—

they raised us to be better than that.

Sisters I'm grateful to,

and would give the world to—

because they mean the world to me.

My two sisters.

Nociception

It signals us to react when we need to —
recoil from scalding water,
and step away from broken glass,
but —
we don't love people that love us,
and love people that don't love us,
and in between that lies *pain* —
we fail to perceive.

Gravity

I heard a 150-pound man would weigh only 25 pounds on the moon,

and astronauts must exercise for several hours a day in space —

to prevent their muscles from atrophying,

and I discerned the greater the size of my ego,

from the distance of my humility,

will determine the gravity of my gratitude.

The Placebo Effect

Stoke a child's imagination,

and place compliments in front of them like stepping-stones,

in a way that will allow them to climb towards the heights
of their dreams —

because the world will sometimes tell them the opposite,

and they will believe it the same —

because the secret is that an adult without dreams,

and imagination,

are children grown up with depressed dreams,

and imagination.

Hieroglyphics

I couldn't read her for a long time —
but when I finally got the message,
the deciphering of her,
became a much fuller understanding of myself —
we can build empires that rival the ancient world,
and rule through dynasties for thousands of years,
as a King is only as strong,
as the Queen beside him.

Terrorism, America.

Can you imagine mob killings of a people mostly by hanging?

Lynchings gruesome enough to make you vomit,

intended to terrorize,

and intimidate a population to maintain a supremacy—

and authorities so indifferent,

that their shared hatred of the assailants,

never obstructed these lynch mobs,

or punished their leaders,

you could see the government's tacit support to the barbaric practice—

3,500 lynched between the civil war and 1960,

victims routinely young black men suspected of contact with a white woman—

do you see why our mothers cringe if we covet you?

It's a trauma seeded in her womb,

not because she doesn't like you,

before getting to know you.

Bodies of victims burned,

bodies of victims dismembered,

castrated,

bodies shown to the public—

I remember the graphic photos of the practice when I was child, people shown smiling next to the charred remains of their victim,

it terrorized me.

It was no *Holiday* when *Billie* sang of *strange fruit-*

lynching,

a homegrown American form of terrorism.

Monsoons

She said she could feel the sadness in her bones,

when thunder struck,

and lightening flashed,

rain thumping against the windows untamed,

wind became microbursts —

that would slap over lofty trees seeded from hope of happiness.

Evoked a flood of emotions,

of when she was lonely —

alienated by the social circumstances,

and mucked memories of the past that made her a maverick —

but he too is a loner,

so,

he lies next to her,

and offers his chest as a pillow,

for her to lay her head on,

to ease her angst in solidarity with him —

when the monsoons visit every summer.

Royal greetings

What up, King?

I can't call it,

I'm getting' money,

What you on?

Thriving.

Yo,

why you always call me King?

Because you always talkin' bout gettin' money,

but you don't even know the king of wealth for all times is Mansa Musa,

a black man like yourself —

study your history,

King.

Exhibition

At least two,

South African Khoikhoi women,

19th century Europe —

rendered freak shows for exhibitions,

Hottentot Venus.

Throngs of people flocked to ogle her bulging buttocks —

they envied what her body held naturally,

tried to explain it with words like "steatopygia."

She died in 1815,

the exhibition continued —

brain,

skeleton,

and sexual organs in a Paris Museum until 1974 for display —

remains finally repatriated for burial in 2002.

Back during her exhibition,

it was exploitive racism,

another way we were solicited as a commodity —

and now her body is emulated to appear more physically attractive,

at the knife of a male plastic surgeon —

he can make you look just like,

Sarah Baartman.

The exhibition carries on.

Libra

Simple sentences,

I'll overanalyze,

and what seems to be a vacillation between extremes —

the only sign that can discern naturally what someone means,

and what they meant,

when they said what they said,

by how they said it —

reading between lines,

and situations instinctively,

for immense clarity on both sides of the spectrum —

it helps me get a better understanding of people,

weighing the scales,

to determine if I want to allow you in my orbit,

or enter yours.

Vampires

Black don't crack,

or maybe it's in the genetics,

the melanin —

the two teaspoons of Sea moss at sunrise,

and hot yoga —

that exfoliates bark complexion,

rejuvenated.

Vitamin D from sun salutations,

we need more than others —

fasting for several days,

the autophagy,

to regenerate.

Ingesting ginger lemon,

and turmeric juiced with cayenne pepper —

the deep breathing.

The negative connotation of the color,

is offset by the power of its properties to preserve.

Maybe the answer is that we are vampires —

we bit the neck of the world,

and everyone wants to look forever young.

Telos of an Acorn

In the cells of a small acorn,

is already an oak tree —

and when we enter this world as infants,

the telos of the infant,

has every form of us along the way of our life journey —

along with our death,

imbedded in our cells.

Each grain of sand,

drops through the hourglass of time,

moving us toward that destination —

consequently,

we're already dead in several ways,

therefore,

what is there to be afraid of in living?

Eternally,

the telos of an acorn.

A Million in One

He was in what he thought was a dilemma,

there was a woman in his life —

she peeled back layers,

opened his eye,

the 3rd one —

from the pineal gland,

he said he never knew he had such a supply,

of strength,

and power to tap into,

but he was growing selfish —

so many women he could weave the physical,

and spiritual with,

tantric.

Baba told him he could have access to a million women,

with what she helped him discover —

or he could access a million women in her,

if he chooses her as the true discovery,

because she chose you the same —

sacred choices,

because maybe a woman is God.

Conversations to the West of me

You looked extraterrestrial to me as a kid,

I got all my cool from you-

a cousin,

but closer to a brother.

I became a better hooper because of you,

a gauge closer to my age,

you gifted me Hip-Hop—

and I stole your *A Tribe Called Quest* albums from your room,

Bonita Applebum,

and *A Love Supreme* are still my favorite songs of all time.

I studied your vernacular,

slang with geek smarts—

a clever way to perplex the "talk white,"

and "too black" prism.

They don't understand your genius like I do,

I'll always look up to you,

the conversations we've had—

for Ayahuasca trips,

over spliffs,

close as Lay's,

and potato chips.

Zenfinite,

Blessed Price,

Observant Servant,

Pondering Wanderer—

the monikers.

The broken record that resounds from your heart's speakers,

from the inception of your parent's divorce at a pivotal stage,

for a black boy coming of age,

you withdrew—

I've been in solitary confinement of my own mind for my entire life,

but I've always had a way to communicate with you,

and we speak to each other when nobody else can.

Like when you're telling it me that you're loosening the headlock of that liquid python—

It's working. Ya boi powering up! 7 days deep. Strict salad and smoothie diet. Big up to Niacin and Vitamin C. By this time next year, I'll be able to punch through a skool bus, throw a baseball through the sun, and do a 360 tomahawk with a medicine ball from the free throw line!!

When your words extol me greater than a Sun's praise to the planet—

You're the Goal of every black man's aspiration. Cool, calm and collected. Keep it funky but exude freshness; spiritually capacious. Wisdom and a heart that's most high vibrations.

Assure me you're feeling better after visiting home—

Powering up, Bredren! Massive Love! Coming home has amplified my mission!

Expanding my consciousness—

Imma send you Yogananda's Energization Exercises that we talked about. My mans Yogananda said he used to meditate in graveyards to overcome the fear of death. That's by far the Hardest shit I've ever heard. Word to the third eye!"

Letting me know our health/growth exchanges we've had are paying off—

Fruit smoothies with almond milk, sea moss, turmeric and cayenne pepper. Been on that Vitamin D! And yo, not only has it curved the drinking. It's eliminated my anxiety and depression as that book said it would. Uhuru!

How alcohol created an intrepid wordsmith who learned to wield words as weapons—

Clowning each other is an integral part of our adopted culture in this terrible country. Another defense mechanism we developed through this horrific experience. I was way too sensitive as a kid. So, I thought. BUT I had the intelligence and ingenuity to melt any nigga that clowned me. Alcohol loosened my lips.

How space is consequential to us both as Libra and Aquarius air signs—

I feel like we should all have the fortune of growing up or experiencing the country, to some degree. Humans weren't meant to live so close together. I'll be damned if I Ever pay a homeowner's association.

You're expanding—

Veganism, meditation, self-knowledge, love thy neighbor, each one teach one. All peaking right now. Leakin' out my grapefruit.

And expanding more—

Last time I had an edible, I kept getting higher every 30 minutes for about 8 hours. Straight astronaut!

Letting me know that the next morning was a welcome back to harsher conditions—

Breath reekin' of weed, Hennesy, and black n milds.

And showing faith simultaneously when I'm concerned—

I feel you. I don't know what to believe. But I know that God is in control of the whole show.

My call was appreciated —

I love how the universe moves. The timing of that was impeccable.

How much I mean to you too —

The one thing separating me from the Emerald city,

you're an integral part to my victory.

And when we attended two funerals for two men back-to-back days,

because they transitioned the same day,

your father and an uncle for you,

and two uncles for me…

I don't how I spoke at both funerals,

you told me how much you still miss your pops,

and to this day I've never heard loss described so clearly —

I was transfixed, and so proud of you. What a time…did they really set sail on the same day?? You honored them both with impeccable perfection. Amazing. I miss him so bad, Marquez. So bad. Still hurts like a fresh wound.

With honesty from your spirit in a way that he can hear it —

Our relationship sucked. But that was my champ. Rest in Paradise, pops. We'll make it right, beneath ethereal sunlight.

With revelations of your travails —

I been wrestling with the devil my whole life.

To switching channels —

Wild memory. A chick I worked with at the courthouse went to school with you. According to her, you walked on water and fed the poor with one loaf. I told her, "That's my Brethren!! He's that niqqa!

And sharing how you did something utterly remarkable —

Circa '99. Left everything behind. Pilgrimage to an ashram. Brother Bimalananda. Direct devotee of Paramahansa Yogaananda. He was pure spirit. Hit me with multiple gems. There was a hoop court there. I instantly became a celebrity. No look passes to monks, splashin' 3's, shatterin' ankles...buckets. It was extraordinary, Quez. All vegetarian meals. I had a job there. It was a self-sustaining community. I learned how to drive a tractor...met people that was really about God!! Like for REAL!! And they all had a definitive spark in their eyeballs, a calmness in their spirit, resounding humility and exuding love/companionship. Met niggaz from New Zealand to China.

And switching again to convert stories to laughter about your father, my uncle —

Pops got suspended for hittin' somebody wit a whip in the 60's. He carried a razor too! Man. That's hardcore. I ain't never heard of a nigga mobbin' wit a whip. Salute Daddy!! You was on some other Gangster shit!!

To commiseration about your ex-wife —

She's fukkin' up my mojo, feng shui, mental health...

Turning to Hip-Hop —

Everybody raps nowadays. Hip-Hop has shaped the frequency of the whole, entire planet.

To the cure —

The Spirit Molecule.

and your finish line in sight —

I've overcome everything from trees, to pills, to cigarettes...that liquor is the last and mightiest adversary...victory is at the cusp!

Ideas pertaining to corporeal punishment—

Man!! I'm so glad that old slave, beat your kids mentally is weaning out. We joke about it, but it was NEVER effective as niggas think.

To Deontay Wilder—

Boi dishin' out that WHAMMO!! If you haven't been sleeping well lately, he got you covered!!

And Anderson Paak—

"I can't roller skate for shit, but that joint makes me wish I could. I would turn the rink out!!

Trips from the past and off to the future—

Yo, you're talkin to a man that dropped acid and sat in a dark closet, to see what would happen. There was mad light in that darkness- I was backstroking in the Milky Way. There's something in the future for us. We're gonna link and level up and shower some power on the planet. I truly do believe that. Migrate and touch all kinda soils.

Because you probably won't come back to AZ—

I don't miss that shit at all. The sun be scorchin' niggaz with a personal vendetta out there.

Giving the last jewel for the night—

Historically. All Saints made that move. Consciously removed themselves from 3D, to be where HE/SHE BE. I honestly believe that the energy I absorbed there has helped sustain my life, through all my terrible choices and behavior. I shoulda died a while ago, Bro. I've seen the light, been to the gate, etc. I've seen and heard Demons…On the flipside, I seent and lived with Men of God. They had a certain twinkle in their eye, and an unprecedented kindliness. Men that were bout that Life.

And hanging up the phone as we always do—

I love you, cuzzo. Always and forever. To infinity and beyond.

Letter to tomorrow

Tomorrow,

know that hope isn't a fantasy,

it's a vital nutrient—

the collective breath we breathe to break-fast when our eyes open,

and we arise from the domain,

where the obstinately optimistic dare to dream chimeric,

and live egalitarian,

long away from the dystopia some have vowed to continue as the ruination of an entire species.

There are footprints on the moon,

hence,

the sky is not the limit,

the mind is—

draw on its well,

and you'll find that doing anything you want isn't a cliché,

it's a matter of you versus you.

What's in the heart,

will come out of the mouth—

in love,

and fury—

and a hurt heart won't hear love no matter how loudly it is professed,

control your tongue,

and shun the tongue when it tries to say negative things
about yourself—

the subconscious is unable to differentiate between the
polarity of what it is told,

for that reason,

make your subconscious your genie by telling it your
wishes,

and positive manifestations will be your reality.

Weaponize your ideas,

they'll live on long after any gun,

sword,

or bomb your hands once brandished—

anyone can kill,

it takes the same hand to exercise greater restraint,

when handling the pain of others personified—

our pain is the killer's killer,

there's no enlightenment needed to know,

that we have been wiping ourselves out,

as a result,

caution yourself in rushing to fight,

for those who do,

expire prematurely,

while the orchestrator grows old to tell the tales of war.

A man's love is life,

and a woman's life is love—

balance both feminine and masculine,

because life is short,

and love is everlasting.

Every person you encounter is your teacher,

the ones who hold your anger,

bitterness,

and resentment—

are your masters,

the lessons are your yogic practices—

every inhale and exhale are backs bowed to offer reverence to moments gifted.

Only grow apart from those who don't grow,

and caution yourself from eschewing those sent to help you grow.

Be comfortable with having enemies,

for there is a thin line,

between enemy,

and friend—

anyone who has all friends,

and no enemies,

is an enemy to themselves.

Learn different languages,

it will allow you leap the borders that the hateful have constructed.

Delude yourself not with money,

it's the liquid tool for living that you can't take with you—

they'll siphon it from your sarcophagus,

therefore,

leave the land for your next generation —

it's the only thing mother earth isn't producing any more of,

the highest value resides in places we call property to house our homes.

Don't follow anyone,

allow the answers from within lead you.

Never look down on the homeless,

that cardboard they sleep on could be your bed tomorrow,

as the circumstances of life are whimsical —

and understand that one man had everything and nothing,

while another man had nothing and everything.

If you chose to see yourself as energy immersed within the universe,

then the universal most high,

will present itself and you will no longer pray to an old,

bearded man in the sky —

and if you chose neither,

your energy will remain indestructible.

Respect all beliefs of others,

but don't allow theirs to cast you down,

to anything fear based when you don't subscribe to them —

because tomorrow,

I'll tell you of a story that my father told me,

of a man who would walk around with a bird in his hand,

asking strangers if the bird in his hand was dead,

or alive —

and if someone said the bird was alive,

he'd crush it,

and reveal a dead bird,

and if someone said the bird was dead,

he'd open his hand,

and set it free —

that man will approach you one day,

and as your father,

I'll make sure that you know,

that the bird is in that man's hands,

and so will be your decisions in life —

when you arrive,

my unborn children.

That John and Yoko

If it ain't that John and Yoko,

I don't want it.

Serendipity can introduce us at a London gallery,

where you're preparing for an exhibition of your work—

we connect instantaneously,

on multiple levels,

artistic,

political,

physical,

spiritual—

they fell madly in love,

John and Yoko—

married on the first day of spring.

I'd leave the most popular assemblance,

of griots for that type of mutual spark with a woman,

my pen would make its bed in a drawer.

If it ain't that John and Yoko,

the Beatles broke up a year later—

my faithful readers could speculate whether you played a role in my separation from the griots,

the stubborn stillness of my pen would still reject the swerve of new words—

If it ain't that John and Yoko,

I don't want it.

We could renew "bagism,"

and collaborate for bed-ins,

akin to sit-ins to protest the times,

you'd probably unfasten my eyelids to a further vison of sensing the world—

empowering me to become my best self.

If it ain't that John and Yoko,

Ono was everything to him—

a woman who helped Lennon transfigure from a self-absorbed musician,

and drug addict,

into an aware activist—

progressing from a deadbeat dad,

and abusive husband from an earlier marriage.

If it ain't that John and Yoko,

I don't want it,

I want a woman to co-create with like a *Double Fantasy*—

we could write the greatest story of love ever lived.

Lennon had a brief affair,

Ono forgave her erstwhile lover after a vamoose,

and 18-month break,

they had a son,

and he retired from music to be a househusband,

and full-time father—

if it ain't that John and Yoko,

see,

she wasn't acquiescent,

and he wasn't milquetoast,

they understood each other on a level to elevate together —

Lennon posed naked next to Ono fully clothed in their last photo,

to make a statement about how we view,

and objectify women's bodies in a patriarchal society —

she frighteningly watched as he fought to say his last words,

after a bullet pierced his throat from the gun of his assailant —

If it ain't that John and Yoko,

I don't want it,

because if I had a woman who wasn't embraced by my fans,

like Yoko has never been after I left,

my love would exonerate her from the grave,

when they blamed her for being a murderer to something they loved,

when they missed the point that our love was greater —

If it ain't that John and Yoko,

let me be,

I don't want it.